STEAM
RAILWAYS

STEAM RAILWAYS

C. HAMILTON ELLIS

Book Club Associates London

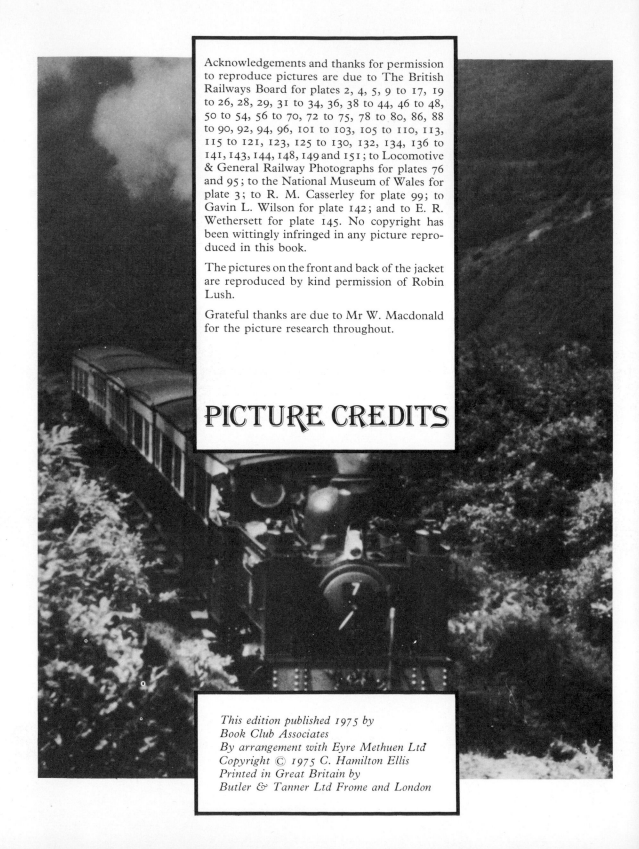

Acknowledgements and thanks for permission to reproduce pictures are due to The British Railways Board for plates 2, 4, 5, 9 to 17, 19 to 26, 28, 29, 31 to 34, 36, 38 to 44, 46 to 48, 50 to 54, 56 to 70, 72 to 75, 78 to 80, 86, 88 to 90, 92, 94, 96, 101 to 103, 105 to 110, 113, 115 to 121, 123, 125 to 130, 132, 134, 136 to 141, 143, 144, 148, 149 and 151; to Locomotive & General Railway Photographs for plates 76 and 95; to the National Museum of Wales for plate 3; to R. M. Casserley for plate 99; to Gavin L. Wilson for plate 142; and to E. R. Wethersett for plate 145. No copyright has been wittingly infringed in any picture reproduced in this book.

The pictures on the front and back of the jacket are reproduced by kind permission of Robin Lush.

Grateful thanks are due to Mr W. Macdonald for the picture research throughout.

PICTURE CREDITS

This edition published 1975 by
Book Club Associates
By arrangement with Eyre Methuen Ltd
Copyright © 1975 C. Hamilton Ellis
Printed in Great Britain by
Butler & Tanner Ltd Frome and London

Posed the question as to which machine most changed the world, the Many will plump for the aeroplane or the motor-car. But it was the steam engine. It came, in practical form, from Thomas Newcomen, James Watt, and Trevithick. With such engines, the Industrial Revolution began.

INTRODUCTION

In the first decade of the nineteenth century, mechanical locomotion by land – and that at first meant essentially the steam railway – not only enabled great loads of minerals to be carried from upland mines to the nearest ports; from 1830 onwards it showed that people also could be moved. Even in 1825, George Stephenson had driven a train on the Stockton and Darlington Railway, on Teesside, on to which some 600 voluntary passengers had enthusiastically crammed themselves. The social beginnings of the steam train were however very mild. The Stockton and Darlington hauled its first loads by steam, but it took its first, cautious, business-like passengers in a sort of double-ended, double-boxed, double-booted stage-coach, horse-drawn between the steam trains.

The timid had to be lured, and that was done in various ways. The railway must be imposing, and respectable, and solid-looking. The timid feared being poisoned by clouds of coal-smoke, so the engines for many years burned coke (which was more lethal as to its gases, but not so dirty). Starting with the Liverpool and Manchester, handsome station buildings had to be provided. The first, terrifying tunnels had to look safely substantial, so, especially under Brunel, they were given splendid portals like castle gateways or triumphal arches. The viaducts looked imposing anyway, but many of

them, too, were embellished with castellations.

The first-class railway carriage, thanks to Nathaniel Worsdell, immediately took shape as an enlarged compound of the road coach, mounted on an improved railway wagon frame with spring-buffers and screw-couplings between each vehicle. That was the prototype of the compartment-type railway carriage, much later to be improved by side-corridor access and communications to all sorts of comfortable amenities. The Americans, by contrast, after dabbling a little with the same form, took for their prototypes the American canal packet for passengers, and the long horse-drawn omnibus. Some European countries went quickly for the American style. Some compromised, or combined the supposed virtues of both sorts. Australia was for long 'English', but New Zealand went 'American', and so did Canada from the real beginnings.

With the locomotive, it was quite another story! Very few people had ever seen one when it ceased to be simply an industrial machine, to become a domestic one. It could not be disguised as anything else! It was large, and hot, and noisy, and oily; a mechanical beast. So England especially (and soon after, America) embellished it, at first with bright and cheerful colours. Advised, one believes, by Worsdell, the Stephensons in 1829 painted their **Rocket** in a bright yellow, with – folly of optimism – a white chimney. Dark greens and dark reds became, however, favourite colours in early days. Lots of polished copper and brass helped. But soon it was not merely a matter of colours and bright metals. Before the 1830s were out,

Sharp Roberts and Company were fashioning their brass dome-casings in a strictly Etruscan style, and others imitated.

So the railways arrived, rapidly after long battles between Radical capitalists who had backed them and landed Tories who had often as bitterly opposed them. And the Great Western had arrived as a *Royal Road*. (It is a pity that other railways were not built like it, on that splendid broad gauge.)

In early to mid-Victorian England, the Great Western and its associates covered a slice of country on 7 ft. $0\frac{1}{4}$ in. gauge, between the northern and southern systems which used what had become the standard gauge of 4 ft. $8\frac{1}{2}$ in. (1.435 m.) initiated by the Stephensons. The Great Western's was a lost cause almost from the start, but it lasted for 55 years. What a splendid way that had been to build a railway!

Locomotives steadily improved, with much higher pressures (a great virtue, at first feared) in the boilers, and the use of steam expansively in the cylinders by ingenious valve gears, notably those of the brothers Daniel and John Gooch on the rival Great Western and South Western Railways, in place of the primitive business of alternate admission and exhaust, as in a simple toy engine. When one century turned into another, the use of superheated steam was about to transform boiler efficiency of big engines, and by then, with the greatly increased weight of rolling-stock, big engines with big boilers had become very necessary indeed, even though, in some places, they might work in pairs (a quite unmentionable factor on the Great Northern in Patrick Stirling's time and much disliked on other lines except in mountain country or, for example, on the Midland Railway which believed in light trains behind small engines, but had to do something about it when faced with a heavy Scotch express).

Increased weights, especially in passenger service, were due to great improvement in passenger amenities. Ironically, that same Midland Railway excelled in these from the middle 1870s onwards, with lovely carriages. The old second-class had been a weatherproof coop. The old third-class had been a tumbril-on-rails, until Parliament in the late 1840s compelled the companies to keep such passengers (a-penny-a-mile, once a day, at not less than 12 m.p.h.) protected against fatal exposure. In 1874 came Pullman cars. Next year even the third-class passengers (on the Midland) had a bit of stuffing to sit on instead of the plain board, and by the late 1880s – though very rarely as yet – they even had that blessing which was a lavatory on the train. Corridor trains first came in during those years. In 1891 the Great Eastern furnished a diner for all classes. The *real* sleeper – at a price – had come in 1873.

Just as importantly came continuous, power-operated, and, above all, *automatic* brakes throughout the train. Were it by ejector-induced vacuum, or by pump-induced air-pressure, it *had* to be automatic! It had taken a long time to enforce for the signalling of trains the *block system*, with electric telegraph communications over each block section so that no two trains could be in the same section at once. Of course there always could be mistakes on the human side. We have not yet escaped them. Rather more than a century ago, railway companies were discouraging mechanical improvement in communications because they thought this would make signalmen less alert.

When old Queen Victoria died, in 1901, the steam railway was rising to the summit of its influence. Trains, at their best, were fast, safe, efficient, unrivalled on land as carriers of freight or of passengers. But there were already electric trains – and trams – lifting traffic better suited to their own means, and in our own time the electric train has come into its own. Steam retreats now, and retreats again.

The object of the following collection is to portray the *aspect* of the British steam railway system, not its barebones history, from the years when steam trains began with the pioneers, to those in which the last of them ran in viable service. Our last great steam expresses ran in the 1960s. The Bournemouth Belle ran to the last under steam, with very dated, and remarkably comfortable, old Pullman cars, 130 years after the first steam express set off from London (Euston) to Birmingham and the North. On that same London and South Western line one of the most eminent mechanical engineers had been Joseph Beattie. He died in 1871, having been born in the year before the battle of Trafalgar, the year in which Richard Trevithick first made a locomotive haul a train. The design of the engines which worked the last Bournemouth Belle in the late 1960s was the work of Oliver Bulleid, himself (a New Zealander) the last, very advanced, Apostle of Steam in Great Britain, and Ireland.

Down the years many great men still steeped in the old traditions had produced splendid locomotives: men like Churchward on the Great Western; his young man who was to become Sir William Stanier of the London Midland and Scottish; Sir Nigel Gresley of the London and North Eastern (Bulleid was one of *his* young men!) and many illustrious precursors in the Victorian Era. Noteworthy is the fact that they designed not only efficient, but *beautiful*, engines. Nowhere more than in Great Britain and Ireland was *style* observed so strictly in the finished aspect of an engine. One could recognise at once that British style. It was everywhere in India, and flourished over much of South America. For long it dominated Australia. It turned up wherever there was, or had been, British influence, in countries ranging from the Netherlands to China. There were many subtle variations, as study of the following examples immediately shows. The Great Western was brassily flamboyant to the last, while the later engines of the L.M.S. were austere by comparison though their features and lines still bespoke Stanier's Great Western training. Bulleid's resembled nobody else's, and some of the *amateur fancy* were terribly cross. Bulleid simply smiled his peculiar smile.

Many people love things for their own sake, outside their work or their art. Of the steam train, one doubts that any machine has had more love from quite disinterested persons. It has been hated, too, for that is a natural corollary with all sorts of things. The late Sir Osbert Sitwell hated horses (having been compelled to the ritual of *Stables* when a boy) and a very eminent Dean of St Paul's disliked music, which was just too unfortunate for a clergyman. Yet lovers of music and lovers of trains are often the same people, whether professional or otherwise. Dvořák adored trains. He was cross with a pupil in Prague who had not noticed whatever engine had brought him in. He himself was missing at an important musical date in New York. They found him, starry-eyed, down at Grand Central (or it may have been the old, marble Pennsylvania Terminal). Both tone and rhythm have something to do with it. Listen to both Dvořák's *New World* and Sixth Symphonies! New York Central in the former and Austrian North Western in the latter (though *that* might have been the South Western between Salisbury and Hewish summit)!

People who love steam trains keep them alive today, fully working, on remoter lines in various parts of the country, both at home and abroad. There never was anything else at all resembling the steam railway. It is unlikely that there will ever be anything like it again!

So, to the Picture Gallery!

Although truly-public steam railways are dated arbitrarily from 1825, with the Stockton and Darlington line in northern England, their beginnings as viable machinery go back 21 years before that, and so we introduce them through their precursors. If Richard Trevithick, Cornish mining engineer, had not produced the first compact, high-pressure, stationary steam engine, he could not have developed it into a locomotive, whether for road (1802) or tramway use (1804). In all three instances,

1825

the engine *went*, to the astonishment and dismay of James Watt, whose ponderous low-pressure engines were hitherto the mainstay of mechanised industry. Watt said in a rage that Trevithick ought to be hanged in advance for all the murders he was liable to commit through explosion of high-pressure boilers. (As it was, this was to be a rarer sort of accident in the long years to come.)

But Trevithick was no businessman. He had *made a train go* under steam in 1804, then lost interest, save that in 1807 he did convey the very first fare-paying passengers, by steam on rails, up in the Bloomsbury area of London, on a circular track at a-shilling-a-head admittance, with a ride for the bold. A derailment quenched his ardour. He died poor. It was left for more dogged prac-

tical mechanics: men like Matthew Murray, Christopher Blackett, George Stephenson and Timothy Hackworth, to bring-on the Great Idea, and for, first, colliery-owners and then shrewd, moral businessmen like the rich Quaker, Edward Pease, in the North East, to finance them.

George Stephenson, son of a colliery engine-man on Tyneside, was illiterate until long after puberty and learned his letters late and hard. But he knew engines, and took mathematics as a duck-

1837

ling takes to water. He became a civil engineer just as he became a mechanical one. He could build a locomotive at the time of Waterloo. He could build a complete railway by 1825, from survey onwards. By 1830 he had built the first railway as we understand the term; with up-and-down roads, complete inter-city public traffic, and steam propulsion, between Liverpool and Manchester.

1. 'Captain Dick' (Richard Trevithick 1773–1833), father of all mechanical transport.

2. 3. Model of Trevithick's first – and the world's first – railway locomotive in 1804. Terence Cuneo's painting recaptures the original engine's trial run, on the Pen-y-darran mining tramroad in South Wales.

4. *Ultimate refinement of the Killingworth type. Locomotion of 1825, Stockton and Darlington Railway. Still extant.*

5. *Locomotive by George Stephenson, Killingworth Colliery, which 'ran' for many years after 1815. Note recessed steeple drive!*

6. 7. 8. Above *is the basic chaldron coal-wagon;* right, *George Stephenson beside the Liverpool and Manchester Railway;* below, *replica of his* Rocket *of 1829.*

9. 10.   *Reputedly the first railway station and
probably the first booking-office: Liverpool Road,
Manchester.* Ackermann's Long Prints *accurately
showed the aspect of the new trains. These took
freight and cattle (with pigs having a bad time!)*

*Between is the primeval railway
booking office.*

These years contained the great morning of the steam railway, after an expanding dawn which had been sometimes brilliant and sometimes discouraging, but always hopeful. It is pleasant that first advances were in Great Britain – slightly ahead of the United States, they being closely followed in the 1830s by the more important lands of Western Europe. France was barely a canvas behind. She had produced a mechanical genius in Marc Seguin.

In 1830, London had not yet seen a steam railway, unless we count Trevithick's jolly

1838

circus near Euston Square in 1807. The first businesslike one, the incipient London and Greenwich, extended from Bermondsey to Deptford early in 1836. But by that time, several other cities had each got at least one, in or from or between such places as, not only Liverpool and Manchester, but Bodmin, Dublin, Dundee, Glasgow, Leeds and Leicester. The steam train had really *begun* in public awareness.

By September, 1838, one could travel overland, under steam, from London to both Liverpool and Manchester; to Southampton in 1840, and in 1841 to Bristol by the primeval Great Western Railway on I. K. Brunel's splendid *broad gauge* of 7 ft. More was the pity that this had not appeared in time to become a national standard; perhaps a world-wide one save in narrow mountain

1848

passes, and mines!

In the mid-1840s came both tremendous boom and tremendous slump in railway promotion, with many fortunes made and innumerable small ones lost. There was plenty of fraud as well as foolishness, but the best of the boom produced many of our principal main lines, at tremendous cost but to lasting benefit, for the Railway Mania anticipated the Motor Mania of the present century.

The benefits and the evils of both have now come home to roost. Both induced great mechanical advance, with new communications also starting on the railway side. Rather surprisingly, the railways also produced a unique phase in architectural history.

11. Electric telegraphy started in 1843, mounted beside the Great Western Railway. Its value was realised by the railways themselves. An early single-needle instrument.

12. 13. Standard- and broad-gauge locomotives of the early 1840s: Sharp's (above) was used in many countries from late '30s to mid '50s. Daniel Gooch's broad-gauge Actaeon *(1841) was on the Great Western.*

PASSENGER ENGINE

SHEFFIELD & MANCHESTER RAILWAY

SHARP BROTHERS & Cᵒ

MANCHESTER 1841

ACTAEON

ABBOT. ANTIQUARY. CŒUR-DE-LION. LALLA-ROOKH. PIRATE. RED-GAUNTLET. ROB-ROY. ROBIN-HOOD. WAVERLEY. IVANHOE.

DESCRIPTION

CYLINDERS. 17 ins in diamr. and 24 ins Stroke. Steam ports 1¾ ins by 13 ins long. Exhaust 3½ ins by 13 ins

BOILER. 11 feet long and 4 feet 6 ins in diamr. inside. Fire Box 5 feet long by 5 feet 4 ins wide.

TUBES. 249 Tubes. 11 feet 3⅜ ins long, and 2 ins in diamr. outside. HEATING SURFACE of Box 126.3. Tubes 1287.7 sqr. fr.

WHEELS. Driving and Trailing 7 feet in diamr. 2 pair of Leading Wheels 4 feet 3 ins in diamr.

FIRE-GRATE area 19.2 Superficial feet.

ABBOT. 8 cwt of Coke and 7½ ins of Water in the Glass weighs Leading 15..4..0. Driving 11..2..0, Trailing 10..19..0

14.15.   Let the Broad Gauge flourish awhile! On the left is Gooch's Great Western Rob Roy *(April, 1855). Below is his 'Alligator' class for G.W.R. goods traffic, first built in 1847. Observe in both the consumate draughtsmanship!*

ALLIGATOR. BEHEMOTH. CALIBAN. MAMMOTH. PYRACMON. STEROPES.

─────────── DESCRIPTION ───────────

CYLINDERS 16 ins in diamr. and 24 ins stroke. Steam ports 1½ ins by 13 ins. Exhaust port 2¾ ins by 13 ins.
BOILER 10 feet 6 ins long and 4 feet 3 ins in diamr. inside. Fire Box 4 feet 11 ins long by 5 feet 3½ ins wide.
TUBES. 219 Tubes 10 feet 11 ins long and 2 ins in diamr. outside. Heating Surface of Box 121.33. Tubes 1134.40 sq fr.
WHEELS. Leading Driving and Trailing 5 feet in diamr. and all coupled.
FIRE GRATE area 18.44 superficial feet.
BEHEMOTH with 7 cwt of Coke and 7 ins of water in the Glass weighs Leading 9.18.0. Driving 10.2.0. Trailing 7.15.0.

16. *Daniel Gooch's masterpiece; the 'Eight-foot Single', dating back to 1846/7 and built-new into the 1880s. Here is the first Sultan (1847–74).*

17.　*Offside of* Lightning, *G.W.R.,* (1847–78). *Note the mixed-gauge rails on the turntable! There were complexities!*

18. *Architectural pride: Newmarket on the Newmarket and Chesterford Railway, 1847. The building has long outlasted the railway.*

19. *Hardwick's superb Great Hall, Euston, London and North Western Railway, 1847. It died by administrative violence over a century after.*

20. *Luminants: Left is a candle-lamp taken by passengers to augment the miserable oil-pot lamps* right *dropped through a hole in the roof.*

21. *Another misery! First-class carriages, as built from the 1840s to the 1860s. A West Midland specimen, very properly* dumped!

22. *More architectural pride: Bourne's drawing of the great engine house, with its traverser, at Swindon, G.W.R.*

23. *Bourne again! The original Temple Meads Station at Bristol, with its superb hammerbeam roof; still extant.*

24. 25. Facts and Fancies: *Above is a fact; that of the impact of the Great Northern Railway below the Boston Stump. The engine is doubtful. Below, a fancy of the old-and-new sort; the engine is a fact. Quite a good representation of the 'Great A' on the Great North of England Railway, by Robert Stephenson!*

RAILWAY TRAIN & TELEGRAPH

By 1849, the Railway Mania was over by some years, though many important lines would yet be planned and built. The old bubble had been pricked by such various papers as *The Times* and *Punch*, and by such people as that distinctly unparsonic clergyman Canon Sydney Smith. In 1875 there was an official Railway Jubilee up in the North-East, having the year 1825 as a starting-line, with a grand procession of locomotives past High Street House, a very modest two-up-and-two-down cottage at Wylam where George Stephenson had been born.

By 1849 it was just possible to travel from the South of England to Aberdeen by railway, subject to several changes. By 1874 one could do it from Penzance in Cornwall to Wick in Caithness, though that was still a long business by what remains the most nearly direct route. In 1849, the best rolling-stock for passengers was still of the compound-stage-coach sort. By 1875, real sleeping cars were two years old and Pullman cars had arrived from America but one year before. There had been tremendous improvements in communications, as in block-system signalling. The motive power had benefited by enlargement and refinement of the basic locomotive, especially as to suspension and valve-gears. Given a good start, splendid railway architecture had blossomed, in the full—and now admired—exuberance of Victorian Gothic Revival, as

1849 1875

at St Pancras. Admirable, too, were the rail-sea connections with Ireland and the Continent, with the railway companies themselves maintaining splendid fleets of steamships.

Steam conveyance had become *respectable*, and in spite of occasional accidents it was far safer than ordinary comings-and-goings in city streets, stables or at sea. Queen Victoria had used the train gladly since her first trip in 1842. On the debit side, only the new, imported Pullman cars could be relied on to keep passengers warm in winter. Minerals and freight went slowly indeed, but much faster than by horse-and-wagon.

Mails were given express treatment from the beginning, very soon with Travelling Post Offices, and, later in the century, exclusive postal trains serving North and West.

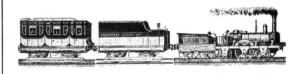

Above *detail of 36.*

26. *Vale of Neath Railway, iron third-class carriage, 1844. (Milk van, 1870; end of miserable career, 1887.*

27. *The classic Allan Buddicom locomotive; a London and North Western example by F. Trevithick. Type built for many other countries.*

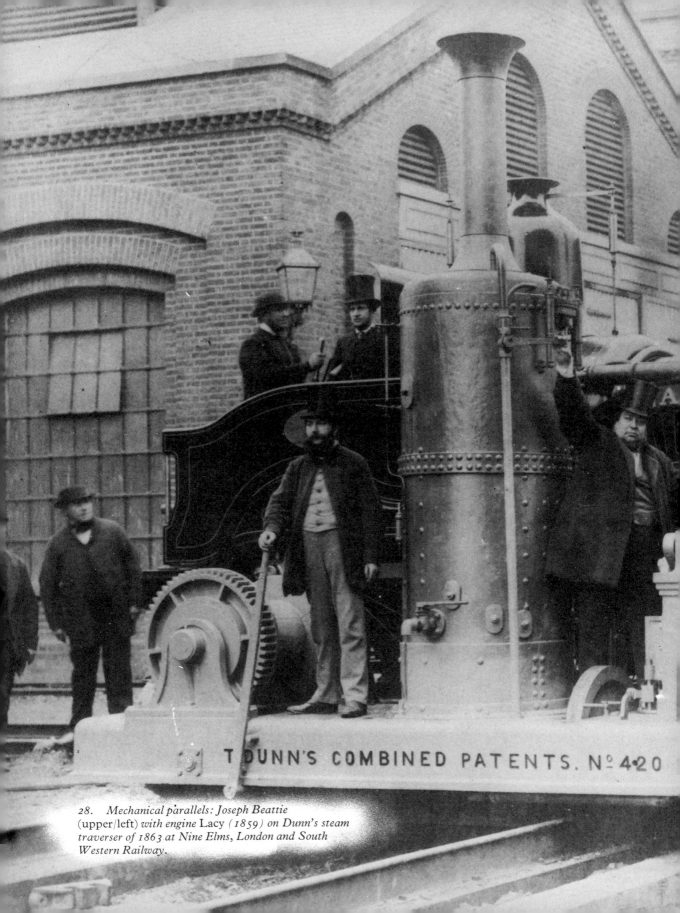

T DUNN'S COMBINED PATENTS. No 420

28.   *Mechanical parallels: Joseph Beattie (upper/left) with engine Lacy (1859) on Dunn's steam traverser of 1863 at Nine Elms, London and South Western Railway.*

29.   *Queen Victoria's day saloon, London and North Western Railway, 1869. Designed by Richard Bore, it has long been preserved.*

30. 34.   *Variety in bridges:* Upper left *is Robert Stephenson's lovely Royal Border Bridge, Berwick, 1850;* left, *some of I. K. Brunel's work, with timber superstructure in South Devon.* Right: *progress and completion of his Royal Albert Bridge, Plymouth/Saltash, 1859.* Bottom left: *Engineers' group during completion of the Severn Bridge, Lydney (early 1880s).*

35. 36. 37. Above: *A veteran rebuilt! Great Eastern Railway, 1860s.* Left: Patrick Stirling's chef d'oeuvre, *the Great Northern 'Eight-footer', built over 24 years for East Coast expresses.* Below: *An ancestress of the Stirling; John Ramsbottom's* Lady of the Lake *for the London and North Western Railway; Gold-medal engine, 1862 Exhibition.*

38. 39. *Broad-gauge in the West: Great Western*
Antiquary *was a sister (or possibly brother!) of* Rob
Roy, *(fig. No. 14). The class was chiefly used on the*
South Wales line beyond Gloucester. James Pearson's
9 ft. single tank-engine for the Bristol and Exeter
Railway was built in 1853. Fleet, but short-lived!
Driving wheels, flangeless; bogies, fixed pivot; rubber
springs. (Left.)

40. *Cliff-fall near Dawlish, South Devon Railway, 1855; passengers being convoyed round; fish-tea in middle foreground.*

41. *South Devon Railway: Tank-engine* Stag. *Her rebuild (or replacement) was one of the last two broad-gauge engines to steam.*

42. *A considerable rebuild: Robert Sinclair's Great Eastern express engine, with boiler by S. W. Johnson and bogie by William Adams; mid-1870s.*

43. *Country terminus: 'Marlow Donkey' about to depart for Bourne End, Great Western Railway; probably in the 1870s.*

44. Above: *Steam tramcars of the 1870s: Swansea and Mumbles Railway (dating from 1807).*

45. 46. 47. *Travelling Directors and Officers liked to be well-done-by, and an 'inspection' was often in fact a railwaymen's picnic. There were no sumptuous motorcars at company's expense in those days, but there*

would be an exclusive locomotive and carriage, sometimes combined in the North British specimen, dating from the mid-1850s. The elegant Caledonian version was even more a train in its own right. A man might own a railway. Captain Peel, V.C., commanding H.M.S. Shannon, owned the Sandy and Potton Railway. His engine Shannon (below) still survives.

48. 49. *Underground: The world's first such railway was the Metropolitan in London, 1863, with mixed gauge.* Left above: *The* Hornet *near Edgware Road;* left below *is Farringdon.*

50. 51. *In the Provinces:* Above, *Chesterfield, Midland Railway, c. 1860;* below, *Eggesford, North Devon, London and South Western Railway, c. 1870. Note mixed gauge track!*

52. 53.   *Gothic Revival: Shrewsbury Station was better than some of Victorian Oxford. London, St Pancras (1868), was grandiose.*

54.   *Exeter St Thomas was good post-Regency stucco (with a lovely timber roof beyond). A South Devon flight!*

55.   The little North London Railway went grandly French Renaissance – or at least Second Empire! Broad Street.

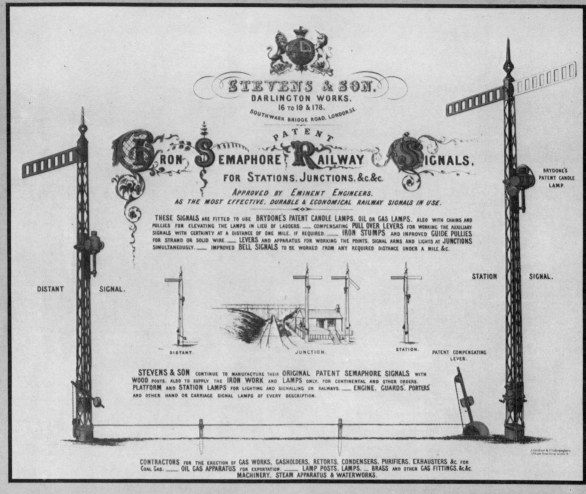

56.   *Semaphores, inherited from early telegraphs, were better than policemen, however disciplined, waving their arms.*

57. 58.   *For a while, disc-and-crossbar served as well. On a common pivot, disc meant 'go!' and crossbar meant 'stop!').*

59. 60.   *What an opportunity was lost, far too early, with Brunel's broad gauge! Imagine a Great Western 'King' with such advantage! These, fore-and-aft, are the extremities of a Gooch 'eight-footer', due to die in 1892. Note the extreme simplicity of the engine's controls.*

In these years came the steam railway's forenoon. The high-noon was to come, and to pass, even though there was to be a sometimes brilliant afternoon, lasting into the 1930s, though with threatening clouds other than those of war, simply through mechanical mutation. The 'Battle of the Gauges' had been unsuccessfully fought through Parliament in the 1840s. Brunel died in 1859, but his broad gauge fought a rearguard action which was to last, bravely, until May 1892.

1876

For better or worse, the British railway industry moved on, making the best of what one retrospectively thinks was the worse job, and on the whole it did so very well indeed.

Not always so, however! Its handling of freight, which save for parts of the south and west of England was its main source of income, remained primitive in the extreme. The vehicles were often contemptible; the speeds scarcely less so. The locomotives indeed advanced in size and power, as they needed to do, towards taking 90–100 wagons with no continuous, automatic, powered brakes, from South Wales to the Metropolis or from the North East to other places. It exemplified the evils of monopoly unchallenged, as did the dreary progress of the 'pick-up goods' in more rural areas. A quarter-century on, the commercial motors were to attack with glee.

1900

In passenger traffic, during these Jubilee Years, there was a much better picture. Vehicles tremendously improved, with diners, sleepers and the prototypes of the standard British corridor train we know. Even in the late 1870s, some favoured third-class passengers were able to *sit-soft*, and the improvement was maintained. There came splendid express engines, achieving famous speeds, with real racing between London and Scotland. The once-loafing South Western came to challenge the mighty Great Western in the West and ran distinctly better local services.

Even on difficult mountainous lines, as between Perth and Inverness, with heavy trains in summer, locomotive performance was often very good indeed.

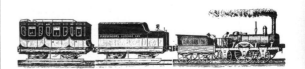

Detail of 82.

61. 62. 63. *The dying broad gauge:* Above, *a convertible engine;* middle, *the* Leopard, *which with the* Stag *was the last to steam (1894);* below, 'Moriturus salutat!' *(one of the last 'eight-footers').*

64. *Paddington, 20 May 1892. The last broad-gauge Cornishman, posed for an obituary photograph.*

65. 66. 67.   *The road narrowed! Left: Conversion or breaking-up! Broad-gauge locomotives dumped at Swindon in the summer of 1892; right foreground,* Warlock*; 'convertibles' conspicuous by their brass domes.* Right: *Prototype side-corridor train by William Dean, Great Western Railway, 1891.*

68. 69. 70. 71. *Great Western signals in the 1880s:*
Left *is the once-common slotted-post semaphore at*
'clear' *(invisible) and* 'danger' *(horizontal) giving*
night indications by white or red lights. Once widely-
used on most railways, clogging of the slot by snow
brought disfavour. Below: *Flag-signalling survived*
during breakdown. Right: *Veteran signalmen (the*
bucket may be classed as office-furniture).

72. 73.   *Country-town stations in vernacular styles: Kidderminster followed the black-and-white English of the Welsh Marches. Great Malvern (right) was and still remains a charming piece of Railway-Gothic, garnished with beautiful ironwork.*

74. *Right at the end of the century, the Great Central came to London as its last inter-city main line. As such, it has died, bequeathing us Marylebone; all red-brick, terracotta and girders.*

75. 76. *East Coast to Scotland, 1890s.* Below: *The Flying Scotsman, with Patrick Stirling's 'Eight-footer' No. 1003 (Great Northern Railway, 1894).* Left: *Third-class luxury; also Great Northern. Note Argand lamps in clerestory and theatre-stall seats!*

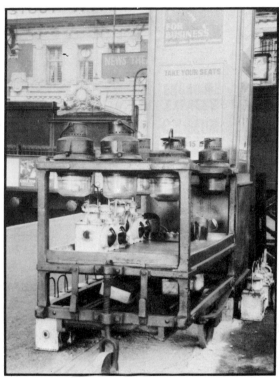

77. 78.   *London, Victoria:* Left, *the then shabby Brighton Side in the 1880s with a Stroudley Class D engine shunting a family saloon and to* left *an aged London and North Western train for Willesden.* Right: *Lamp-trolley on the Chatham side; carriage lamps above and train tail-lamps below. Picture more recent than might be guessed!*

79. 80. 81. 82.　Above: *King's Lynn in the 1890s: Private engine* Gazelle *in front of Great Eastern No. 0706, which it long survived at Longmoor Camp, Hampshire. Below, Manchester Sheffield and* *Lincolnshire No. 147 (1884).* Opposite: *Tank- and express-engines of the Eastern and Midlands, later Midland and Great Northern Joint, Railway, in the 1880s.*

83. 84.   'All stations to . . .' The Great Western 'slow' is coming into Bath behind an old express engine (by Joseph Armstrong) in the 1890s, with the outer, broad-gauge rails still in situ ; the London and North Western one is headed by an equally venerable express-goods, of John Ramsbottom's 'Special DX' class.

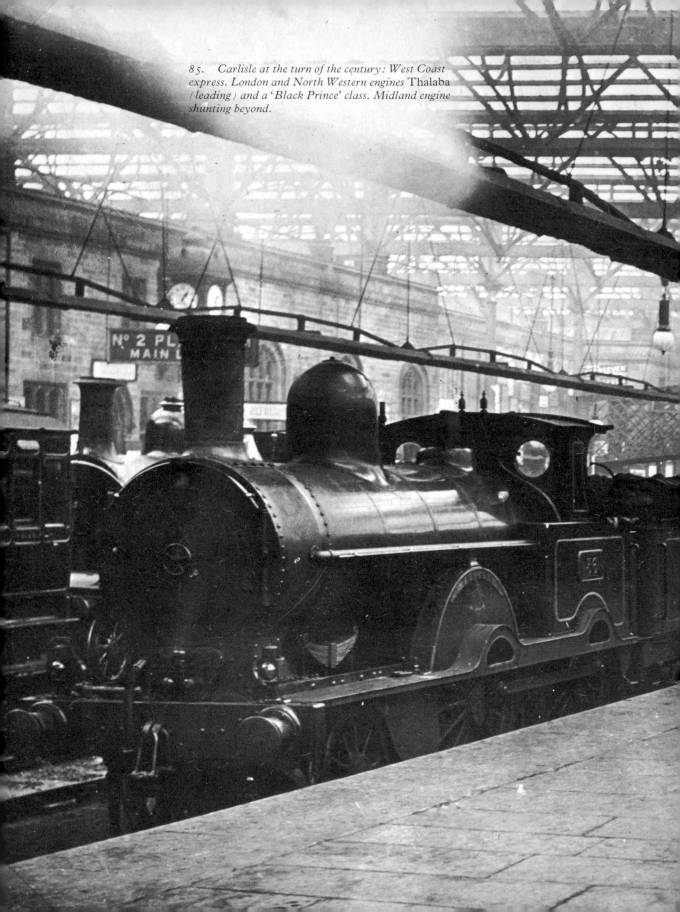

85. *Carlisle at the turn of the century: West Coast express. London and North Western engines Thalaba (leading) and a 'Black Prince' class. Midland engine shunting beyond.*

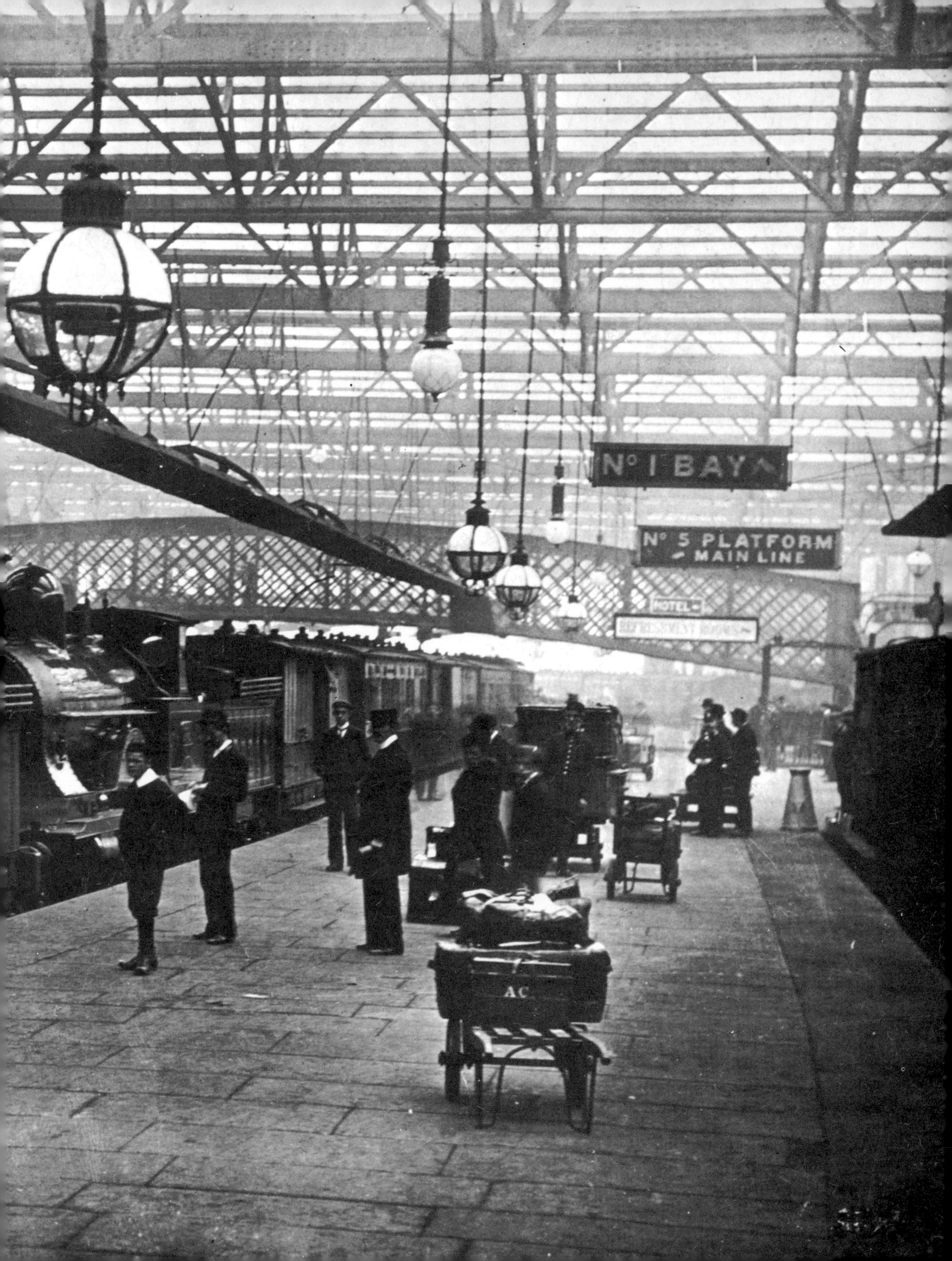

Nº I BAY
Nº 5 PLATFORM
MAIN LINE
HOTEL
REFRESHMENT ROOMS
AC

86. *North Eastern express engine No. 548, 1866–92, before rebuilding in 1885.*

87. Below: *Caledonian Railway No. 123 was in the Race to Edinburgh of 1888 when two years old. Now lovingly preserved.*

8.   *North Eastern No. 779 (1887–1930) under the
d North Bridge at Edinburgh Waverley.*

89. 90. '*Exhibition run' on the last night of the Race
to Aberdeen, 1895: London and North Western
Hardwicke (which survives) and Caledonian No. 17
each* averaged *67·2 m.p.h., from Crewe to Carlisle and
from Perth to Aberdeen respectively.
Driver Soutar in command.*

91. 92.   *Narrow-gauge:* Above *is the Glyn Valley Tramway, a canal-feeder which nevertheless carried passengers until 1933; engine* Sir Theodore. *Below is the Festiniog Railway, oldest public narrow gauge in the world; opened in 1836, with steam since 1863.*

93. 94. *Provincial and Continental.* Below: *Midland Railway train, with a 'single driver', leaves Gloucester for the North.* Left: *London Chatham and Dover Railway's Continental Express is scheduled to reach* *Dover the same minute as the South Eastern's, running from Victoria and Charing Cross respectively; crossing here at Bickley.*

95. 96. *Western rivalries:* Left: *an Adams express engine heads a London and South Western train to Waterloo, at Lipson Junction, Plymouth.* Right: *a Great Western Plymouth express from Paddington leaves a Brunelian tunnel portal, that of the 'Short' just east of Box.*

97. 98. *City contrasts:*
Above: *Earl's Court, London,*
District Railway, in 1876.
Right: *climbing from Glasgow*
Queen Street to Cowlairs,
North British Railway, at the
end of the century. There, cable-
assistance up 1 in 45 lasted until
the early 1900s.

Queen Victoria died in 1901, and 14 years later the Victorian Era died too, an early casualty in consuming war. Those years saw the proud glory of the scarcely-challenged steam train. Motors were largely a preserve of the rich; aircraft were either sporting or military, for few thought of them as being viable in business. The railways' only serious enemy was the electric tram in closely-built areas. There *was* the motor-omnibus; there were few vans and lorries. Progressive railways

1901 1914

indeed sponsored the new, and fallible, sort of bus *as a feeder* in remote places. It could reach the Lizard from the Great Western. It could reach Braemar from the Great North of Scotland. The Great Eastern even *built* some of its own; all for places with no trains.

Heavy freight and minerals all went by train. Anything from great expresses to the *Thirty-nine Stops* (a later sailors' name for the train from Inverness to Thurso) knew no serious rivals save the private cars of the well-to-do user. Against the tram, and the new tube lines in London, a few companies essayed limited suburban electrification.

Elsewhere, the splendid steam express reached new heights of magnificence. Locomotives grew and grew for, with new and sumptuous vehicles, trains became much heavier. Higher pressures, superheating of steam, and improved front-end design, as well as much bigger boilers, were in

very truth *heap-big-medicine.*

For the best – and a lot more – of the traffic, it was still *one-driver-one-engine*. The driver had the pride of a skipper, commanding his fireman and his regular cleaners; obeying Rules. Driver Gibson of the Caledonian mounted a gold sovereign amid elegant filigree work on the regulator of his engine *Cardean*, working the 2.0 p.m. Glasgow to London, and its corresponding northbound train from Carlisle, which was the 2.0 p.m. out of Euston, late in the evening. The companies painted their engines and vehicles in gorgeous colours – blue engines on the Caledonian, crimson on the Midland, green with lots of brass on the Great Western – and so-forth, with splendid heraldic *insignia*.

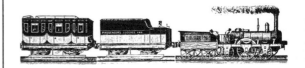

Detail of 113.

99. *The real Ireland, as recently as 1961! The British gave steam railways to the Irish. The Irish gave to the British some of their greatest locomotive men, as from Joseph Beattie to Richard Maunsell. The nations were different. The railway tradition was the same. Here is a chartered trip by the Irish Railway Record Society on the then-dying Cork, Bandon and South Coast line, appropriately headed by a C.B. & S.C. 4-6-0 tank engine of Coras Iompair Eireann, on Innishannon Viaduct, Co. Cork.*

100.   Railway in the Townscape:
High above Folkestone stretches the
old South Eastern main line.
Costumes are about 1930, but the
train is vintage South Eastern and
Chatham!

101. 102.   *Narrow-gauge, living and dead: British Railways only steam line today, in the Vale of Rheidol.*   Right: *the still-lamented Leek and Manifold Valley Railway (1904–34).*

103. Engine Bessemer *with the Sunny South Special
(Manchester–Brighton) near Balham in 1905.*

104.   *Engine* Ant *brings down the quarry trams.*

105. 106.   *Against falling local traffic, railway companies produced 'rail-motors' and 'auto-trains'. The former (a South Eastern and Chatham example) was a combined engine and carriage, possibly with a trailer. The latter involved an old engine, with two control-trailer coaches in this example from the North Eastern Railway, which with unconscious irony called the outfit a 'twin-autocar'.*

107.   Above: *Great Western inspection train.*

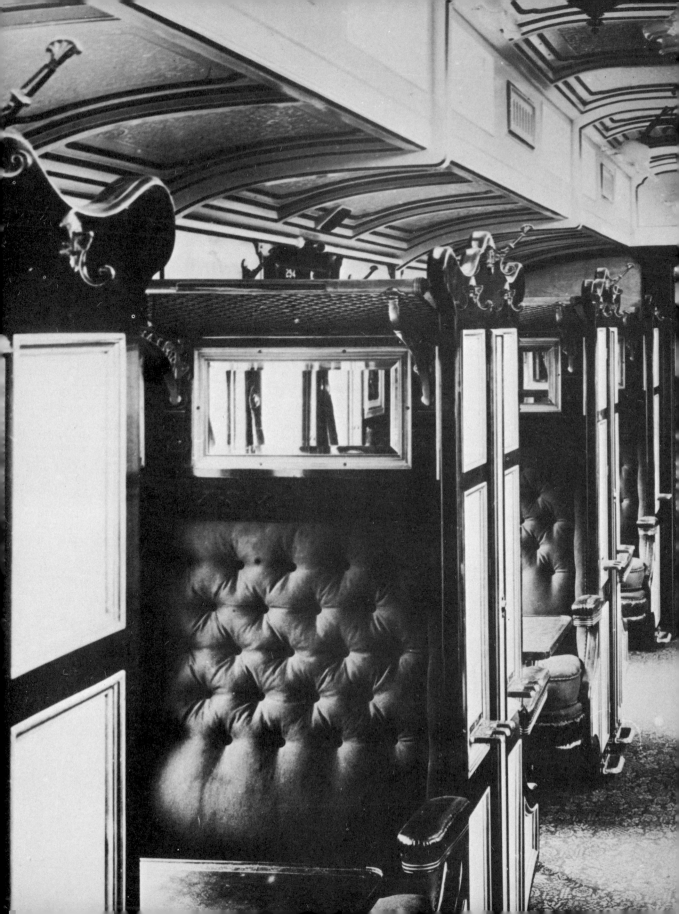

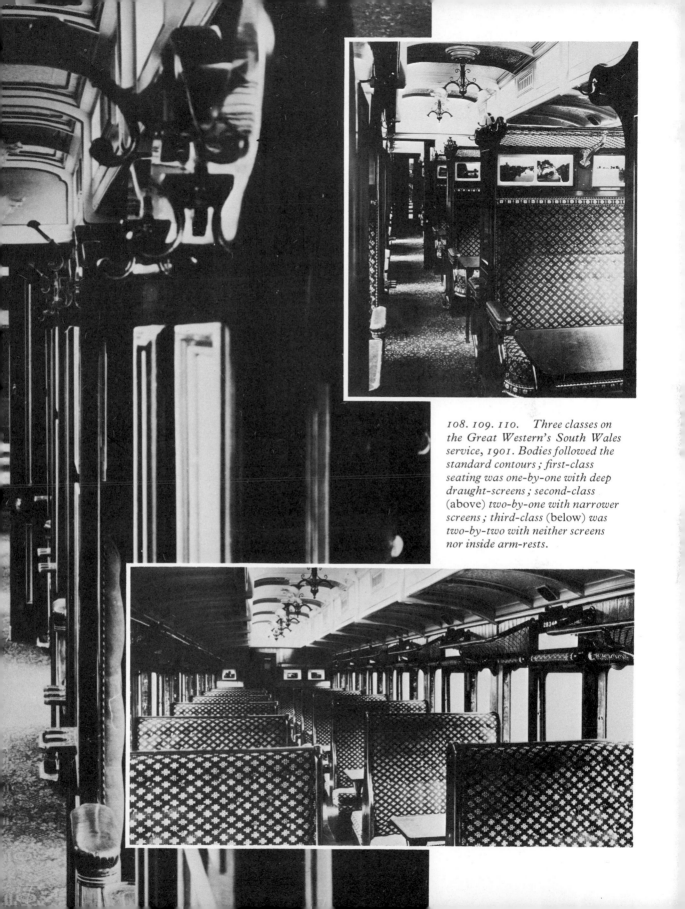

108. 109. 110. *Three classes on the Great Western's South Wales service, 1901. Bodies followed the standard contours; first-class seating was one-by-one with deep draught-screens; second-class (above) two-by-one with narrower screens; third-class (below) was two-by-two with neither screens nor inside arm-rests.*

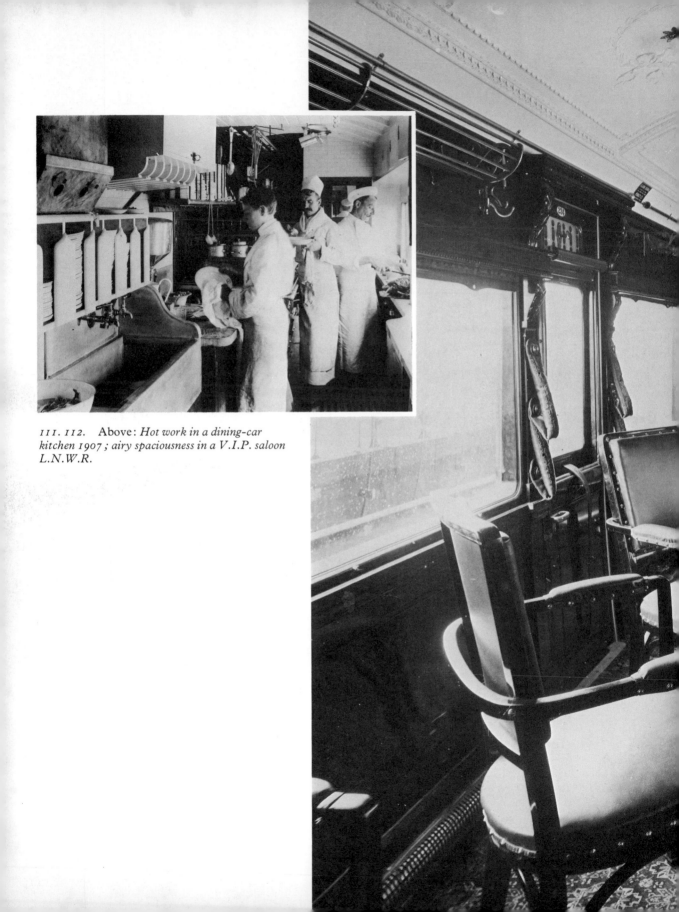

111. 112.   Above: *Hot work in a dining-car kitchen 1907 ; airy spaciousness in a V.I.P. saloon L.N.W.R.*

113. 114. Below: *Cold work for the postman with mail-exchange; first used in 1838.* Above: *French's balanced semaphores (long used on the Great Northern).*

115. 116. 117. 118.   Firstly, Scottish pride and
provision: Left, *the 2.0 p.m. to London at
Glasgow Central, with the fabled* Cardean
*(Driver Gibson); right, Caledonian engines on
parade (Dunalastair IV class); middle-right,
the Highland Railway's Strathpeffer Spa Express
(engine* Loch Maree). Below: *The new ally and
later challenger – Great Western motor-buses
paraded outside Slough Station.*

119.   Departure from Paddington, G.W.R., to the West, in 1904. The man on top of the train is filling lavatory tanks. The ladies' coats suggest a chilly spring morning. Note sawdust on platform!

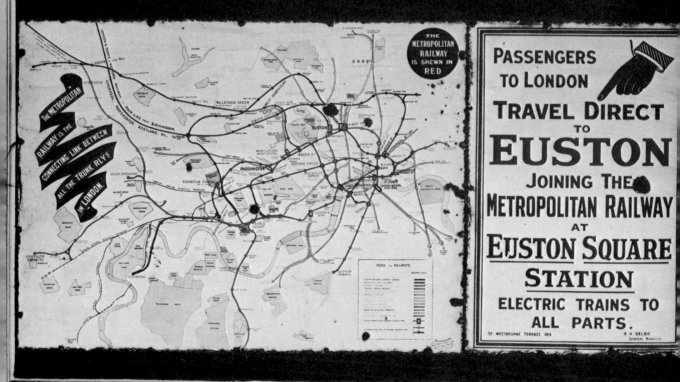

*120. 121.   Edwardian railway publicity: The Great
Northern's (above, left) excellently reproduces one of
its expresses, while adding some improbable mountains
above Hadley Wood. The Metropolitan's (below, left)
is admirably factual.*

*122.   Horses had given motive power to railways at
least since 1602. Here is the last Great Western
shunting horse. The last Great Eastern one died,
appropriately at Newmarket, in the 1960s.*

Forty years after the English Railway Jubilee, all the British railways found themselves under state control, though not yet ownership, which had been provided for long ago, in the event of emergency, by the then young W. E. Gladstone. The decade ended with the first Railway Centenary in 1925, and a situation in transport as changed as was the social one. In the war years, the railways were worked down to their bare bones, with maintenance and replacement

1915 1925

low. After it, with de-control, Government did its best to bilk the companies that had served it (the doughty North British, very hard-up, fought it with ultimate success, though posthumous as to the company itself). For in 1923 all the old main-line companies were grouped into four big, more or less regional ones, which was reasonable. While the war had seen stultified mechanical development on the railways, it had furthered immense development in motor transport, and, helped by successive railway strikes from 1919 onwards, the motor moved in, itself helped by an enormous release of Government-surplus lorries. The airliner arrived too, though rather sportily than as a serious menace, starting with converted bombers. In remoter places, the little railways, some of them on narrow gauge, were about to die slowly, one by one.

To this part of our record, let us add a sort of *enclave*, containing several periods

with the likenesses of uniformed railway staff. Railway uniforms came from two sources: firstly from the Police, and then (an inspiration of Admiral Moorsom of the London and North Western Railway) from petty-officers and warrant-officers of the Royal Navy. Hence the dark-blue serge. When British Railways went into grey, there was wrath and bad-language. For higher officers there was the bowler hat with a dark suit. 'Come on! You're us! It sticks out a mile!' said a ticket-collector at Sheffield, waving two visitors from the Great Eastern through his barrier. *Directors receiving Royalty, and station-masters at some of the great city termini, wore silk top hats. Even the frock-coat died hard!*

123. London and South Western ticket-collectresses, c. 1917. The company's tailoring department meant well!

124. 125. Above: Aberdeen commuters on the Great North of Scotland Railway. Below: First class on the Great Western, middle 1920s; milk-chocolate broadcloth and gold-lace.

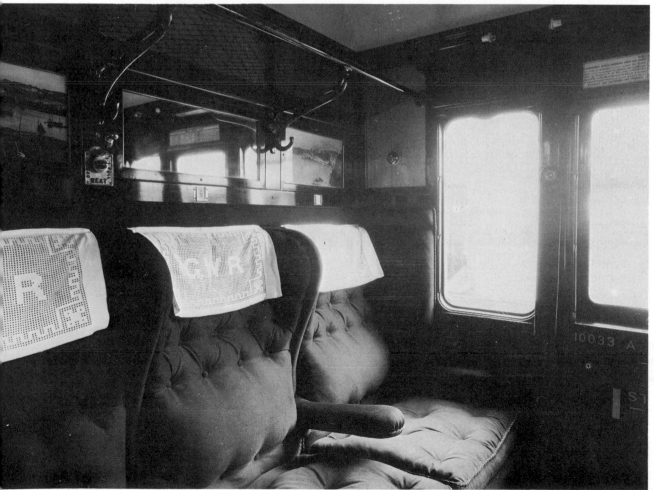

126. *Signals: The mechanical locking frame, dependent on heavy muscular effort as well as intelligence, concentration, and highly sophisticated electrical safeguards, was to last for a very long time yet. This was Reading West on the Great Western.*

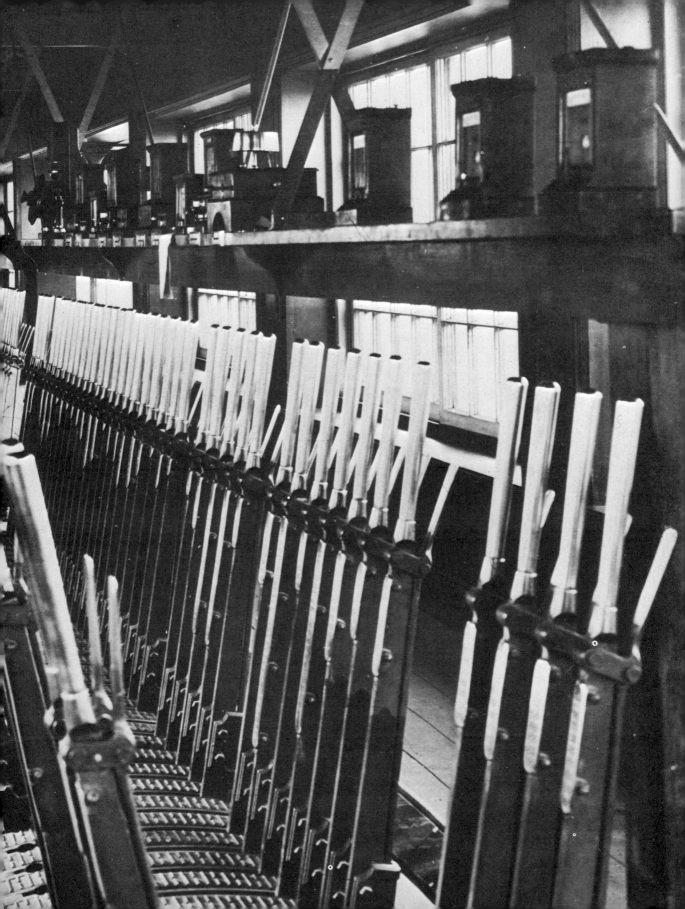

127.   Two engines back-to-back with two snowploughs likewise; a North Eastern patrol for the Pennines in winter.

128. 129.   *Contrasts – as ever:* above *is the last train* | *first train to Lynton in 1898. Both outlived the North*
on the narrow-gauge Lynton and Barnstaple line in | *Eastern engine* (below) *heading the Queen of Scots*
1935. Leading engine, Lew, was built for the Southern | *Pullman train out of Edinburgh Waverley, and built in*
Railway in 1923; her elder sister, Yeo, had hauled the | *1922. The Lew ended her days in Brazil.*

130.　*People again, and we go back a long way!*
Young porter of the Eastern Counties Railway,
c. *1860.*

131.　*Visiting inspectors with a hand-car; mixed-*
gauge, Great Western country, 1860s.

152. *A veteran with his fighting-cock at Olton, Great Western Railway, near Solihull, Warwickshire.*

133. *South Eastern porters. The deplorable third-class carriage was still around in the 1920s, improved by gaslight.*

PUTNEY & · · · · · ·
CLAPHAM JUNCTION·S·W·

Van Trolga

134. *London and South Western Guard. He
frequently wore a rose in his spare button-hole.*

135. 136.   Above, *a London and North Western, and below a South Eastern, guard.*

137.   *Midland Guards: Changing fashions from Victorian* (left) *to post-Jubilee* (right).

138.   *Royal Guard David Hughes, M.V.D., of the Great Western.*

139.   *Mrs. X . . . sweeping-out the London and South Western, about 1918. Her tight-lipped look is understandable.*

These were critical years! Triumph and disaster, menace and recovery, with final decline, as of an old Monarch or an old General! Machines have perished like personages, to be admired thereafter. So with the viable steam train in Great Britain.

In 1926, there was a General Strike in sympathy with striking miners. The trains stopped. A few soon began to weave through chaos. Miners at Cramlington derailed a fortunately crawling Flying Scotsman. The engine turned over with drunken-looking carriages in rear, before a jeering audience of men and women, but there were only a few black eyes and bruised joints. Inside a fortnight it was over, but by then some of the gullible were convinced that the train was not absolutely necessary, thanks to the efforts of those who knew how to drive a motor. Not for the first time, the commercial-motor stooped as a hawk on ready-made prey.

In the 1930s the railway counter-attacked, with steam trains haring along at 110–120-odd m.p.h., here and abroad. In 1939, once again, a way of life collapsed. Motors were for war and essential business only. Back went vast traffic to the rails. But in spite of streamlined expresses, the companies were somewhat out-at-elbows. Government compelled them to a beggarly deal, based on their worst previous results, and took control. They swallowed their gruel and fought

1926

their war well. Government collected railway profits beyond its dreams.

Nationally viewed, perhaps that was as well. It was an awfully expensive war. The railways emerged with little-trumpeted renown, otherwise direly damaged and much worn-out. The State took over in 1948, to be sometimes imaginative, but a fickle master, and often mean. Steam traction died, slowly; electric traction – now from Dover to the Clyde – came slowly while the oil industry's darling, the Diesel, was furthered on both rail and road. In the 1970s came an *oil crisis* which may be lasting a long time, and the more humorous of the gods laughed. For the rest, people still work steam trains for love, as they sail for love, whether in ships or in post-Montgolfier balloons.

THE END

140. Water-trough pick-up; originated by Ramsbottom on the London and North Western before 1860.

141. 142. Above: *British Railways, Western Region, went on being visibly Great Western at least until steam died. Here is* Montgomery Castle *with the South Wales Pullman at Paddington in 1956. Below, and in 1950, a Glasgow–Inverness train crosses the Baddengorm Burn arch near Carr-Bridge behind one of Sir William Stainer's 'Black Fives' (L.M.S. of the 1930s).*

143. *Thames Valley snow at Taplow. Over many years the South and West could catch it as severely as Sutherland or Buchan.*

REFRESHMENT FACILITIES
GREAT HALL - CAFETERIA & BUFFET
PLATFORM 13 - BUFFET
46151

44.   *Old Euston, as recently as 1953.*

145. 146.   Above: *The* Mallard *at King's Cross, L.N.E.R., in 1938; holder of one of the two world speed records for steam.* Below: *The ex-L.M.S. train,* The Royal Scot, *near Harthope; engine* City of Lichfield, *in the 1950s.*

147.   Southampton in the 1950s, with a Bulleid Pacific below high-piled semaphores. Our last steam main line.

148. *The Southern's Golden Arrow leaving London Victoria in the 1950s, just before electrification to Dover.*

149. Left: *Evening Star,* last steam locomotive built by British Railways.

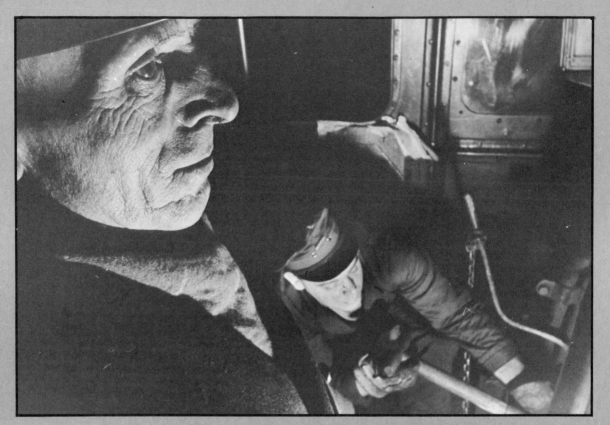

150.   The faces of the Steam Men.